WHEN
FLOWERS
SING

OTHER BOOKS BY *a thousand flowers*®

Everyday Mermaid
Skeleton Woman: A Dance with the Dark

WHEN FLOWERS SING

A POETRY ANTHOLOGY

EDITED BY *Christina Isobel*

CURATED BY *Christina Isobel* & *Trinity Blyth*

a thousand flowers

PUBLISHED BY *a thousand flowers*®

P.O.BOX 1559
SEBASTOPOL, CA 95472
www.athousandlflowers.org
info@athousandflowers.org
FOLLOW US ON SOCIAL MEDIA @athousandflowersbooks

PRINTED BY *IngramSpark*
ISBN 978-1-949824-05-6

LIBRARY OF CONGRESS CONTROL NUMBER: 2023952167

COVER ART BY *Vera Kober*
DESIGN BY *Monique Comacchio*

Dedicating this book to the hope that WHEN FLOWERS SING will deepen our experience of flowers, deepen our inner life, and deepen our connection to the earth. May these experiences awaken ourselves to the urgency of working, consistently, for the health of our planet.

For my grandchildren Huxley and Bronte and daughters Arwen and Meara – my heart.

— CHRISTINA ISOBEL

CONTENTS

FULL BLOOM

FROM LOTUS TO LOTUS

BECOMING FLOWERS

This poetry odyssey of flowers can give you another path into the primal mystical, miraculous, mysterious land of flowers. Flowers are given in every aspect of our lives: births, graduations, courtships, weddings, friendships, illnesses, anniversaries, deaths. May time on this poetry path deepen your pleasure, your solace. May it open you more to the munificence of flowers.

May you hear the flowers sing. They wait for us.

Enter …
to the land of flowers
where lips brush petals of
velvety petal perfect pansies
in purples and blues
gnarled yellows, gnarled pinks
of snap dragons …
Songs of scarlet poppies
clear the air
and my mouth wants to sing
what is there.
Softest pale pinks
thrive on
in naked ladies …
I want to nestle my nose
in the spicy dew-drenched peony.
Hints of scent from
sweet alyssum …
And the whites – ginger lily, gardenia, tuberose, jasmine –
that stop you cold.
Your tongue swells in
your mouth so full
you don't know which is which
taste or smell.
Falling apple blossoms
peppering the ground …
And the roses! spiraling
to your core wafting
colors, perfumes, sound
with pricks of thorn.
All proclaim
Beauty Beauty Beauty
while breaking open your heart.

Christina Isobel

BLOSSOMING

The Flower Shop

I want to open a flower shop on Orange Street
Fill it full of perky poppies and
Dahlias that look like fireworks
Butter-soft roses wrapped up inside themselves
Spotted tiger lilies; an edible spectacle
I want a secret garden on a street corner
Contained behind glass windows
Blooming orchids shyly peeking from
Behind bundles of baby's breath
And breezy foxgloves jingling
Anytime the door smiles wide open

Flowers can mean so many things, you know
One might stop in for a cheerful bouquet
For a special anniversary
Another may ring the bell on the door for
A funeral arrangement, or an ailing loved one
A vase full of apologies for a broken heart
Or perhaps a colorful selection
For a budding infatuation –
It's impossible really, to know just the number
Of memories to be made with
A flower shop on Orange Street

It seems a good path, even a noble one
Not unlike the others, not unlike
The physician or teacher
All of us part of the bigger spinning wheel
Giving and giving, and for those
Who still have hope, caring;

But perhaps a flower shop is
A little softer, a little kinder
A little less sterile and formal,
A little less by the book
I want to open a flower shop on Orange Street
And fill it with people who need love
In whatever form it may be

Kristyn Lee Pankiw

Passionflowers and Miracles

The Gardener says that flowers are called to prove the
    existence of miracles.
Coming clean from the dark earth, they bring us something
    of such exquisite beauty
that even our finest artists can only imitate. They scatter
    grace along ditches and roadsides
with as much gusto as they adorn royal gardens, bringing joy
    to all they meet.
Never striving to be anything than what they are, lily, iris,
    and daisy do exactly
what they are called to do, which is to be the most beautiful
    thing in the world
that is in their power to be.

When we were children, we were amazed by perfumed
    passionflowers that greeted us
like a carnival along the fence outside the Spanish Mission we
    passed on our way home
from school. Enchanted by the bright pink blossoms, we
    drank their nectar,
hardly believing how sweet it was, always returning to taste it
    again and again
to remember. When we traveled later to my grandparents'
    country, we ate in cafés
with plastic flowers on the tables, and it struck me that this
    must be the beginning
of evil: trading what was real for a fake, what was alive for
    something lifeless.
Who dreams of a plastic flower rather than the real thing? Not
    the birds or bees
whose work it is to carry greetings from blossom to blossom,
    allowing those rooted
in the ground to mingle and bear fruit. Behold sunflowers
    and poppies, lavender and buttercups

drawing in winged wonders from far and wide in the living
    world. Even in a tiny garden in a city
by train tracks and junkyards, they come. What we need to
    do is keep our eyes open
for beauty, as hummingbirds do, faithfully returning again
    and again
to the places they find nectar.

There was a man in England who calculated the
    mathematical probability of miracles.
Given that each is one in a million, he found the number of
    seconds to reach a million
and resolved we might expect a miracle each month.
    Doubtless, countless flowers know this,
in their immeasurable grace, and show us that miracles
    happen not just each month,
but every day, and all around, defying all the odds. The
    hummingbird knows this,
and knows what awaits him in his search for passionflowers
    and miracles, tasting their nectar
each time as the first time, its sweetness beyond words.

Nico Arcilla

Flowers in Bloom

I like them yellow and uncomplicated:
Waiting to be picked up from the corner store
Until some broken heart or happy soul
Comes looking for comfort,
Or just to make their joy grow.

I bring them home when I feel alone
Or trapped
Or incapable
Of changing things small or large,
Hoping the beauty of the flowers will overtake
The confusion, indecision, the disarray
In my home.
They will sit there – safe and quiet,
Bring together the yellow rug and the blue mug,
And make sense of the
Coffee left over from the morning –
The black lining the sides of the ceramic,
As if mourning the end of my morning;
Abruptly interrupted by the arrival
Of the 9 am bus.

It was a Thursday after work.
I was still a cog in a giant wheel,
Moving and turning like a hamster,
Running faster and faster.
Trying to make sense of life,
Trying to make a life.
But there was no end in sight –
Whether it was the collective human suffering
Or my specific malaise

And incapacity to create change –
Things looked bleak
And it felt so wrong to speak
Of my troubles
When the world was essentially in a rubble.
Who was I to be so sad on a bright day
In the middle of May?
When you're supposed to be happy and stay
Sane under a warm sun.

But the reality was so much more muddy.
My thoughts were turning cloudy –
Instead of dreaming of a happy Friday,
My mind was thinking about the many ways
In which we could all be gone –
Explosions and exodus
Confusion and delusion,
Delirium and death.
There was no hope in my hurting heart –
Heavy with self-hate, feeling tied down by the weight
Of my inability to make change …

And that's when I saw them.
Contained, containable, clearly beautiful.
Uncomplicated and yellow.
Soft and pliant.
Loving and comforting.

I had marched with a few women that morning;
All strangers that came together
To fight against a shared danger.
And, seeing those flowers was just what I needed

To remember we were in this together.
In a weird way, where no one knew anyone,
People came together for everyone.

Just as the flowers did.
Wrapped neatly in clear plastic,
Each leaf lightly grazing the other,
The geometric mishmash of long cylindrical stems
Keeping them from falling apart.
Delicate yellow buds,
Lightly open, smiling at the sun,
Waiting to fully bloom,
To embrace the world with an upturned face,
Petals slightly parted,
Helping you forget terrible moments
And compartmentalize them as "already
departed."
Ready to remind

Of beautiful memories tucked away in your mind.

I had to have them.

And so I took them home,
Letting them sit in the nook of my arm,
Balancing them against the bag containing my life –
Laptop phone wallet keys.

And, so, I go on home,
I walk into my mess:
The stress and distress strewn all over the floor,
The clothes piled up in the shape of my depression,
The miles of unmet bills,

Unfinished transcripts filling
My home from carpet to ceiling to window sill.

But with the flowers in my hand,
I could take a stand.
And turn my Thursday around
From bland and untamable
To simple and attainable.

And so I let them float in water,
Hope held between petals of mortal beauty.
Just a moment of delight
In a world gone to hell, where friends fight
Grand world events unspool
And create a disgusting cesspool
Of death, destruction, desolation.

But right here right now,
These flowers are in bloom.

Divyanka Sharma

Odessa Flowers

A weeping willow was
My best friend
In Odessa
Where my mother washed
Floors on her knees and
My father sold
Polish jeans off trucks and
Played cards to pay
For being Jewish
I wonder now
If bombs shake her catkins loose
And do her flowers weep and weep
For her own soil as I do?

ZZ Jelenic

Me-Nots

Every year in Spring I look for the
forget-me-nots on that hillside, on the
leeward side that tumbles into the
valley in a slip of green, shimmying
the goods for all to see.
Mary Oliver says, *Beauty is not only
for us*, and I haven't heard a truer thing.

Climate scientists are striking all over the
map today, albatrosses calling a panicked
alarm, they are smart and know
where the land ends. The police are arresting
some, caging the warners, 100 guns to 4 sets of
eyes. The small and blue are truly perennial, may
they cover the ground in hope, may they fill the
skies as guides.

Jessie Zechnowitz Lim

While Listening to Love Supreme

I am meditating on Iris, the flower,
the buttery yellow paint stroke,
beacon of bright to bumbles
in flight. Against indescribable
blue-violet canvas of standards
three. Your blue-grey iris, I dive
into the opening of its black hole,
disappear. In this place, a shore,
the misty sky, color of your eyes.
Paradise is a shore in the core
of your right iris. A wild field
of irises peek through tall beach
grasses on spacious sand dunes.

Did you know there is a field
of flowers living in your eyes?

Remember our bridesmaids,
carrying a lone iris in the dark
theater where we were wed?
I see you all aglow & smiling
as I make my way to you.
That was the day, perennial
wild irises seeded upon dunes
inside your eyes & grew, & grew,
& grew. Did you know: Irises,
like Psalms, like Love Supreme,
are the only surviving things
that live at center of dead, imploded
stars. Such love cannot truly be seen
by all. It shines on over eons & dies
bursting bright to black, then hides
beyond gravity, beyond time, & fuels
us, each ephemeral, fragile being for Eternity –

Kiki Johnson

After Rilke's Roses

The heart is an artichoke, am I right?
The butterflies and moths
are exiting the pages!
If you say it just that way,
releasing them one by one
from the artichoke.
Hey, I was like you, looking up love
in the dictionary like some
heliotrope of higher feeling –
until language just choked
VLKUBOOM
and the heart was handed
its electric nerve petals.

Sierra Nelson

Ode to Flowers

The earth will be saved by beauty
— *Fyodor Dostoyevsky*

Addicted to beauty — flowers
are my drug of choice. Without
them, I will jones and feel bereft.
Even when broke: a newly
divorced, yet to be employed
single mom, I would buy a dollar
fifty bunch of daisies or a single
gardenia for my hair.

I am a sucker for anything adorned
with flowers: dishes, print dresses,
potholders, pens. I use floral soap,
household cleaners, essential oils
and creams. Embroidered tablecloths
bloom pansies and violets. A painting
of peonies, one of torch ginger, poster
of Georgia's poppies nourish my walls.

Cabinet knobs flaunt tiny bouquets
recalling an English nursery rhyme.
Uplifted to sacred space — by the
blooms outside my door: jasmine,
gardenia, plumeria, rose. I thank
them each time I pass: their sweet
fragrance, the blossoms for my
flowered porcelain vase.

I have always felt kinship with flowers,
even with weeds that bloom from
cracks in the pavement. Somehow,
anywhere flowers thrive feels holy,
consecrated for love. Ethereal, with a
delicate whisper, they can inspire the
highest vision of ourselves, open us
to the vast beauty of our own hearts.

Carol Alena Aronoff

Floral Energy

I leap from bed to seize the dress! All winter it hung on the wall, a work of art: black chiffon exploding with resplendent roses; red & pinks. The perfect floral pattern: riotous rose garden, gone to seed, or the brothel's flocked wallpaper in an old western. Matte lipstick matches the filmy silk scarf, blood red and long enough to die like Isadora Duncan. I wrap it about my head and bare shoulders. Dark curls escape. Cat eye sunglasses complete the Italian starlet effect. No time for gelato. I'm late for class. Top down. Music up. I am an embodiment of the season, not quite come. In the student union, I spot flowers, a flier, so I sign my name.

I bring packets of seeds: poppies, daisies & a wildflower mix. His ex brings freckles & naturally curled lashes. He has a type. The over-do it type; busy busy busy bees. He's soft for showy bloomers; for perfumed petals and deep roots, always reaching.

Picture a dreamer who volunteers to plant flowers. I wave: "Hey! Iris!!"

Aptly named, she lifts her head.

I do an awkward jig, crack a joke: "Fancy meeting you here. It's been forever."

With urgency, as though I'm wrong, Iris rushes:

"Just last night you wore your dress, the whole ensemble, billowing scarf and cat eye glasses. You knelt to plant roses and they exploded, growing wild in hyperspeed, bright pink and taking over. They became technicolor cartoon roses, undulating multidimensional fractals growing across time and space. Into the future. I tried to come closer but the flowers were too powerful."

Dia VanGunten

Mizuage (水揚げ)

April
an invitation

embezzling spells
of innocence,
verges of awakening,
Gordian loopholes
from the love language of
hands quietly smoothing over
the crumpled brows of dawn
anguished over what sparse
things it is able to carry
to full term
and leaving the rest
to the condoning shadows.

Believe, somewhere,
in the dulcet hum
of airtight bud lie lyrics
to a lascivious song,
strains of scintillating sins
stroking it into bloom.

It is sometimes not enough
to flower, but to flower for
the first time. Watch her face
for the movement of moments
as if every flush and quiver
charts a map of places
in the order they are touched.

It is sometimes not enough
to sit next to the perfume
of the truth as it unravels,
but to crush the petals in
your own hands and be stained
by it. Call the hunger
what it is: a nuanced torture,
invocation of our mortality,
dark rhapsodies of ache
to remind us we are
evolved from savages.
She would wear all the labels
like a crown. The posture
of her espoused darkness
is the love language of
virgin honesty catching fire.

Becoming resplendent.
Becoming the hunger.
Skin on skin.
Divinity on desire.

And the force and eloquence
of her consent slowly
undresses the world.

Iris Orpi

Pink Camellias

these pink camellias might be
a twitch in the chest
fire in your cheeks
Solnit calls it blue
that endless distance between
the ocean
and a linen sky
call it love
but never write such a thing
oh cliché, cliché, cliché
darling
but what's a cliché
if not the hardest
truth

Gary Reddin

Gathered ~ Wilted

There is a language that nobody speaks but everybody understands.
It smells like rain until it
smells like a daydream.
There is a body of flowers holding their faces toward the sun. Hearing tales of self-same
creatures all coated in pollen and perfume.
Someone I love is grieving.
I don't have the words. I don't speak the language that can make it evaporate.
But I understand as a tangle of blossoms and stems leaves my hand and enters theirs.
I understand the moment when they bury their nose into the bloom and the smell overtakes them.
I understand that the senses act before the mind.
I too have stood in the kitchen staring at crumbs, urging myself to eat when my stomach has
turned to stone. I too have lost my hearing at the supermarket when the sound overwhelms me.
I too have felt the world turn to plastic.
There is a crack in the grief that is flooded with flowers. It is small, almost unable to be
observed. The smell will soften, the leaves will wilt, and the grief will move through them over
and over again.
They will know I picked each one thinking of them.
When I leave (grief is exhausting) my fingers still carry the scent.

Niki Dreistadt

Residence in the Rain

Sitting on the shore
of Fitzgerald Lake
height of the lavender
water lily bloom
just as it begins to rain

the sound
rising from silence builds
to an all-encompassing
gamelan

torrent's
soft mallets
play lily pads
striking flower-petal
xylophones

rain refuses
our being separate
denies us autonomy
draws us in
to become part of its story

passing through
silver veils
we enter stillness
of canyons
inside of the rain

astonished
to discover
in most ephemeral
of dwellings
such boundless shelter

Richard Shaw

Lavender on My Forehead on Ash Wednesday

for R.T.O: *forsan et haec olim meminisse iuvabit*
— Vergil's Æneid, 1.203

if i could smell this moment forever,
i would. as soft & sweet as the strip
of unworn skin between your fingers
you let me idly graze like grass in
sunlight. my nose is cold with winter
but my chest is full of springtime. i
realize now why you're so easy to love:
you're the cherry blossoms in union
square. ever fleeting. so frustratingly
impermanent that i have no choice but
to drink you like rainwater. i don't know
if it's possible to love you like this for
that much longer. my lungs might burst,
blooming too soon, like my father's. i
can't say whether this much loveliness
is sustainable beyond a mere season; we
are two too restless for change. but for
right now, you smell like home. please,
let me soak up all of you, even just for
one minute. & perhaps — as per the son
of love swept from troy — it will be pleasing
to have remembered these things one day.

Tova Greene

Of Hummingbirds and Fairy Trees

Lily of the Valley, your beauty be
under hawthorn trees, hummingbirds nesting
in the thorny brambles of the fairy tree.
Beltane sowing soil with lovers resting.

Hermes slows his hasten flight, finding shade
from spring's afternoon sun, sips sweet nectar
Tatiana shares from her cup, flowers braid
their hearts together, this day a specter.

Purity longs to be quick forgotten.
Gods and Queens subject to eternity.
Duties beckon from skies above, rotten
expectations sours their time – such pity.

Lily of the Valley, until next spring;
our lovers part like hummingbird wings.

Anastasia Helena Fenald

An Offering

Coral-hued daffodils,
Like pink lucky charms
Drowning in the sweet milk
Bath of morning's warm glow
Swaying across green
Carpet, bristled with drops
Too tender
Notwithstanding the sudden
Shake of sunlight stirring
The breeze, and the birds
Plucking soft fat squirms
From haloed earth
Like it's a plate of
Easter pickings

Kristyn Lee Pankiw

March Fourteenth

Dried rose petals

orange ombre and pink

Clink as they fall

and make a crisp sound

like salty potato chips

Zoe Van Gunten

Transmutation

young ceramicist
shaves from the main clay body
crepey wet petals

Boston Haskett

To the Flower Garden

blush pinks, duckling yellows, forget-me-not blues, raspberry reds ...

there is something about the softness
of a single petal
the way it curves around your finger
scent descending
lingering fresh
with the delicateness on the brink of life
with the fragility on the brink of death

this is the petal way

it beckons you beyond the flower gate

Christina Isobel

FULL BLOOM

ROSES

Rosa

Divine Feminine.
Soft as velvet; red as blood.
You are eternal.

Courtney L. Black

Rose

Spring's
green flame
parts
lips

then
its tongue
delectably
licks

Richard Shaw

Roses

layers of petals
cupping
one another
such that
no one notices
how artfully
they protect
their core

Valerie Wong

Lovestruck

aromas of you,
climb up like Eden roses –
misting my marrow.

Pamela Loperena

The Lover's Melody

Rose stems in a half glass full
Glimmering lights hung door to door
Jazz echoes under the hollow floor
Sitting in a paisley chair

My eyes they wander,
To the lovers on the street.

My eyes they remember,
That I have a love
So sweet

Hold him, before he goes
Warm him, before he goes,

Give him all the flowers in this world

Tara Obregon

Our Losses Are Softened

The rose once bloomed and watered
now faded and crumbled
dried petals pressed
between two heavy things,
the intrusive thorns dulled.

The petals threaten to disintegrate into dust –
the edges smudged into something soft
and delicate of the past.

Time does not heal.
It only distances us
from memories
that abuse the mind.

And I wonder – did we not
crush ourselves into this fragility?

Deirdre Garr Johns

A Brief Romantic Daydream

once a month i go to the corner store
the one with the grand opening flags still fluttering
and the mangos that are too expensive.

i pass by on an unplanned walk that is actually
very-much-so planned, like always.

and i pretend i have a lover who i want to buy flowers for.
i pick up a bouquet, one that i'd like, like always.

i sniff it romantically, then i put it down, like always.
i cannot justify buying a bouquet for myself.

i scrape together my change, already counted,
and buy a mango and a single rose.

in a few days' time, my rose is dried and dead
but i put it in a vase anyway with the others.

i like the idea of lone roses finding each other again.

Adrianna Jurek

If All The Wood in the World

If all the wood in the world were to sing

and every rose gave a political speech

and every cloud took pity on its neighbor

and every stone composed an epic poem about
being a stone

and every dust mote were aware of its
mortality as it lay or drifted onto the
curved or flat surfaces of things

and the blind archer let go of his bowstring
and his arrow sang out its target as it
flew through to its intended goal

and the air itself through which it flew
hummed in anticipatory monotones

and water blew wet kisses to the sky

and every flame danced Flamenco
stamping itself out with its own heels until quenched

and each of us saw God direct with our
own eyes in naked vision
as clearly as we see ourselves stooping to
drink from a lake

cupping the water with our hands and
catching our eyes looking back at us
as snowy mountains go up around us to the
peak of the sky

And each of us knows we see this and
acts upon it

and phones ring with the news

But there is no news

It's as old as God

though there be no time with God

and everything is therefore inside-out to
what it seems

and that raw inner surface is
where our existence lies

singing to the clouds and roses
and the blur of things as well as their clarity
and everything stops though it
never stops but only

flows or floats or seems to stop and start so
fast it's like movement but is immobile

as only God moves

though He be motionless

Daniel Abdal-Hayy Moore

Listening to Roses

Have you ever
received advice
from a rose
whispering
through
majestic magenta
puckered petals,
clouds hanging
overhead?
Droplets are beautiful
against the flesh,
she says.
She is valiant
even on
the gloomiest of days.
So, you stand
in the rain
trusting this
downpour
will make you
bloom
just as bold.

Daisy Franco

The Power of Roses

Sometimes, it comes in a rush, this need to remember
the place where kestrel, swallows, koi, turtles, and lily
pads alight at the center of my city. I close my eyes
and I am back, hungover, in full squint under Saturday
sun. Shuffling along 8th Ave with DB. She was a friend
who understood the power of roses. The night before,
my self-medicating existence ran like an iron skillet
into my partner's wounded sorrow and frustration.
Not quite domestic violence but close enough. I left
for the bar, self-fulfilling all his barbs. DB let me crash
with her. And, early morn, next day, there we were,
nauseated and caffeinated like two pros. "Let's go
see the roses. Bring your new fancy smartphone."

It was June, 2009. We schlepped to the Botanic, a good
mile away. Sweating out the booze, getting mosquitos
sloppy drunk. I start clicking away at all the sober beauty
in our own secret Brooklyn Garden. DB and I didn't need
to talk much, we let every row of newly bloomed rose do it
for us. This row: A nod to the hurt-your-eyes-yellow of Graham
Thomas, Harison's Yellow, pepto-pink of the Kazanlik,
Basye's Purple. We turn the corner into the deadly, fragrant
Felicia, Mutabilis, that dear slinky China rose in her pale-
yellow shift, drawn and quartered Boscobel, the rarified
violet of Veilchenblau sharing the arched pergola with a shot
of Variegata di Bologna, the sprawling Damask Ispahan …
then, just there, at row's end, wilting New Dawn. I lost it.
How could anything alive be that delicate and bruised?

Yet, what softest, pink freshness. DB grabbed my hand,
nudged me to the Cherry Esplanade and plopped us down
on lush green carpet, between the red oaks. Lying there, splayed
like Vitruvian man, astral projecting to the Brooklyn blue sky
and back – little girls on a teeter totter – we slept off the last of it.
I think it was then, that very blister in our space-time continuum,
when we made an unspoken pact between touching elbows. To sober
up for good, swallow the sky until its blue dyes our pride and awakens
the expansive voices so long buried in bottles and fliptops. It took us
a minute to mean it. But I know now it was that day, that glorious summer
day, when we rose to our perennial bloom and found our blessed way home.

Kiki Johnson

Bee and Rose

The bee is in a hurry, but the flower isn't.
She is floribunda Betty Boop,
Edging her golden petals flirtatiously with pink.
Frantic in the center works the bee,
Bent double with her effort in the pollen.
Her black thighs, ridiculous as Popeye's,
Twitch among the sweet brown stamens,
Fragrant and warm as pound cake in the oven.
Even her buzz is muffled up in rose.
She doesn't even hear the blue jay's call.
I've found such holy portals, too,
Where pure work crosses into heaven
Through so much beauty.

Anne E.G. Nydam

BOUQUET

Wisteria

Here I am, blue & petal-soaked,
labile as a toddler trembling
in liminal steam, on the brink of growing
murderous, an untamed vine, I am twining
round words unspoken, choking
out the light, daring the dew to drown us
both. I once thought I could be a tulip,
elegant and refined, slim and smooth
and contained, fenced and happy, an exemplar
cultivar, rich in blood and long-lived even
when cut. But that bulbous head was lit
like a flame. I know now I am a wooden
wisteria, strong enough to kill a plum
tree with my sheer tenacity. I am practically
invisible in winter, storing up my insults, then
bursting fat with clustered rage in the late heat
of May. I am always climbing, branching further,
my whiplike tendrils waving for something to slap.
You are a creeping rose, but I cannot twist into you,
you, so sharp and stealthily biting while your victim is
enamored with your scent. My power is not pricking, my
draping saponin is not to be ingested, my skin is not to be
broken. No, I will not hurt if you train your touch, marvel
at my gifting pods, soft and spiraled with a fuzz of fruit, I can soften.

Jessie Zechnowitz Lim

Mademoiselle Neon Noir

I'm feeling silky
Like gentle moonlight milky
Coasting swiftly. I'm drifting.
Through a dreamy color spectrum
That gives a melatonin kick like Beckham

Mademoiselle Neon Noir
My petals radiate like an untouched reservoir.
My pollen will pull you in to exhale
The atmospheric air of mountains afar
And I glow
So much that I'll show
You how to oscillate between the fleshtones
Of the sweet Pacific deep & moonstone

So drink from my midnight nectars,
Surrender your fears to the eternal sky
And let's go.

Sunshine Lombré

The Lavender Plant

The lavender plant you gave me this spring
withered and dried, I forgot to say.
It's brown and bare and dead, poor little thing,
though it is pleasing watching it decay.

The lavender plant reminds me of you,
gifting me flowers smelling oh so sweet,
calming my nerves, a comforting perfume,
fragrant wafting blossoms lull me to sleep.

The lavender plant needed love and care
my sunflower soul did as well.
I could've loved both, my heart wasn't there,
I chose to love myself, and said farewell.

The lavender plant is out of flowers,
weeds take over and slowly devour.

Sarah Blakely

Pink Carnations

Mom's Sacred Pink Carnations,
Pink for a girl, and she was my girl.
Vivid, rich and graceful hues,
Vibrant, lush and lovely, blooming softly
blanketing my girl for eternity.

Mom's Sacred Carnations hailed her strength,
her will power, her witty uncomplicated warmth,
her undeniable faith.
Regal, not pretentious, but dignified,
welcoming, spiritual,
was Mom.

With gentle cheerful ease she lived
with effortless purity,
before her passage to Eternal Rest.
Mom's peaceful transition
was not in doubt.
Was just us two, so perfection there must be.
It was all I had left to give
To my sweet girl.

Gloria S. Lanzone

Jasmine

This is the hour when blooms unfurl, thoughts of my
loved ones come to me. The moths of evening whirl
    around the snowball tree. Nothing now shouts or sings;
one house only whispers, then hushes. Nestlings sleep
    beneath wings, like eyes beneath their lashes. From
open calyces there flows a ripe strawberry scent, in waves.
    A light in the house glows. Grasses are born on graves.
A late bee sighs, back from its tours and no cell vacant
    any more. The hen and her cheeping stars cross their
threshing floor. All through the night the flowers flare,
    scent flowing and catching the wind. The light is now
on upstairs, shining gently out, then dimmed ... It's dawn:
    the petals, slightly worn, close up again – each bud to
        brood, in its soft, secret urn, on some yet-nameless good.

G.E. Schwartz

Scent of a Memory

you sold *atr* for a living

to collect fragrance
you must first soak the flowers in water
then separate the essence
drawing out the oil in darkness

Jasmine reminded you of home
floral notes betrothed to star-shaped clusters
the pride of Damascus
before your world was uprooted

teardrops on the shop floor mingle with
scents of musk/amber/deep rose
how much pain is reminisced
by each bottle

your daughter laughs
as she dabs perfume
on her slender wrist

Jeanelle Fu

Happy Again

Let's put daisies
In coupes of champagne
String them along the
Strands of our braids
And place them in tiny
Crowds of three against
The just-whipped frosting
On a buttercream cake
Let's tuck daisies
Behind our ears, cup them
There for a moment until
We hear the ocean ringing
Loud and clear
Let's stir daisies into
A fresh-tossed salad
Winking amongst arugula greens
And let's line them up
Atop a hot brick wall
Watch them wilt into a melted
Smile from the sun, unless
The breeze whisks them away
Too soon, just for fun
Let's pick daisies
From quintessential meadows
Or cracks in the sidewalk
It doesn't much matter
As long as we gather them
Between pinched fingers,
Plucked gently enough
To leave behind
The stem, and let's be
Happy again

Kristyn Lee Pankiw

From the Shakespeare Garden

— after my mother

Summer sweat licks me as if I am a sepal stretching
open to morning dew as spring dies for the year.

I wonder if my mother's necklace will corrode
as salt slithers between the laced metal holes —

her heart pendant rests on my collarbone,
and I worry it will green or brown like leaves in the garden

as the dew point and sun negotiate what will wither.
A year after the funeral, I visit the Shakespeare Garden,

slouching on a scaly bench that says
"I'll note you in my book of memory."

I often feel more like the soil, a container of roots,
and water slithers up ducts and through my eyes to project

her condensed self from the ground back into life.
I know the garden's orange and purple flowers by color

and not by genus. I know their gaze from Central Park
and from the cemetery. I know their droopy petals

will not uncurl beyond just one season.

Rachel Hill

Parts of Us

Kinnikinnick
Lady Slippers
Paintbrush
Shooting Stars

She taught us to know their names.

Fuchsia
Sweet Alyssum
Vinca Vine
Delphinium

She always remembered all of their names.

What's this one? I asked.
Clematis, she said.
Clitoris? I asked.
Young Lady, she gasped,
hands to her mouth.

Lobelia, she said.
Labia? I asked.
Very funny my girl, she said,
hands to her cheeks.

Begonia, she said.
Too easy, I said.
What do you mean? she said.
Vagina! I said.
Good Lord, she said,
hands to the air.

Bleeding Heart? I asked.
Too sad, she said.
No way, I said.
Lady in a Bathtub, she said.
It's happier, she said.
Oh Mom, I said,
hands to my hips.

Then she was gone.

Plant the ones she liked, my daughter said.
Good idea, I said.
Bleeding Hearts? she asked.
No, I said.
Too sad, I said.
Lady in a Bathtub, I said,
hands to the ground.

Courtney Lowery Cowgill

Late Summer

you can have your daffodils
narcissi
and tulips
fill your garden if you will
with the straight-stemmed
and proud-petaled.
I too once opened the soil for their bulbs
and I nurtured dahlias
and braced sunflowers as they grew
I fussed and cooed over roses

but now
not too late, I hope
I've given in
given up what I took to be my pride
embraced what once I spurned.

Give me loose-limbed and frowsy petunias
give me the soft and rangy ones
with blooms like out-of-fashion hats
unrestrained
and generous as a courtesan
named by her enemies
Petunia
the sound of someone spitting
Petunia
not a name for a flower
but Petunia
I'll be unfair to you no more
no modest or elegant flower
holds me more in her power
than the rude and languid petunias at my door.

Bob Engel

PEONIES

Peony Attempts

a tight closed
bud
ripe with possibility, the color dense
rich.

unleashing petals upon petals
unfurling, billowing, reckless abandon, paper thin, fading
always.

an embarrassment of riches
a flopping featherbed,
a pile of the softest kisses,
the shimmer of delicate skin – private,
a giving up of fragrance,
petals succumbing to
time and age.

a reminder to all women
to be full and brave
over and over again

Jana Cerny

Peony Double Etheree

Why
do I
feel alone
when I look at
peonies? Why do
they get to open, show
off vulnerable insides?
White trumpets thrusting, pink petals
feathering, perfume permeating
into the depths of me uninvited.

A flower heady with its own fragrance,
with its own open weight, forcing me
to at least smell something nice, at
least soften somewhere in my
body. What body of
stalks grows this green? Who
blames them for their
brilliance? Beauty
stabbed through
eyes.

Samantha Kolber

Peony Revelry

The three peonies
brought inside
from the garden
last night
now slowly open
their buds

unfurling
windowsill-bound
they release
a cavalcade
of bewildered ants

their pilgrimage interrupted
as the sweetness
nestled inside
those densely ruffled petals
escapes

I catch a whiff
this morning while
making tea and toast
and I am instantly transported

to Nanny's backyard
loud with
busy chickens
full of sass
scritching under her ancient peony hedge

Polly Hatfield

Pink Peony

An embroidery of black ants
– as tiny as sugar granules –
glide between lacquered petals,
smooth pleats
and rosy satin folds.
Nourished by thick warm air
and rain: soft and precious,
the abundant green leaves are slick
with innumerable translucent beads.

Angela Sloan

Ant Advice

While exploring a garden I saw …

an ant
wandering
   through
    grass
     leaves
      soil
       earth
        as I do.

While toiling in a garden I noticed …

so many
paths
twists
turns
decisions

one   one
corner a   corner of
grassy   buzzing
wetland   bees
of small   pollinating
crawling   floral
life   life

but which one is right?
which path should I choose?

I ponder —
perhaps
the ant
is wiser?

For the ant does not toil or overthink.
The ant lives free and keeps moving in
      sync with the earth.

While exploring a garden I understood ...

paths are distinct
yet all full of life.

    Any path will come
    with both joy and strife

        no right or wrong.
        So, like an ant

            just choose and
            allow myself

                to naturally
                bloom.

Tyler Lenn Bradley

63

Peony

is there any such mystery
as a peony in early summer
budding and bursting,
its sickly perfume adding depth to the monotonous
garden of delights?

the peony is no simple flower.
when it opens, it breathes with the sun,
drawing into itself at night
and hosting a hundred tiny ants
who nestle in its folds,
intoxicated by the smell.

i knew a girl once
who held her cards close to her chest
who smiled at inside jokes
only she understood
who, beautiful and glowing
at golden hour,
whispered poetry in my ear
and challenged me to recite,
whose essence was so unusual,
it attracted the unusual sort.

the boys in men's clothing
the old men yearning to be boys
the art appraisers
the collectors
the secret-keepers
and the perfume samplers
who tried to bottle her exotic mystique.

like ants they clustered
and fed on her
and she gave them refuge

and i know she too
lit up with the sunshine
and cried by the moon

and when i comforted her,
she said not to worry
that her love was a two-way street

but even the fullest peonies wither in a week.
so much majesty needs so much
and will never ask for it.

when in time she fell,
the ants moved on
to another flower
or to the dank hole from which they came
having lost nothing but a soft place to sleep.

maybe, i heard her say once,
this is the best i can get.
maybe there's something wrong with me.

i didn't say it then
because i didn't know the words
but i know them now

i would have said
you are lovely
living, breathing, peony

you are full and unapologetic and wild
and the garden would not be the same
without you

and anyone
would be lucky to hold you close to their heart
anyone
would be lucky to wear you as their crown,
nestling you softly in their hair.

a bouquet of you
is breathtaking,
even a single stem of you
is enough to make anyone smile
and when you retreat into yourself in the moonlight
you are no less breathtaking than in the day
for every being needs its rest.
sweet peony, you are no different.
you are more than a home for insects
you are more than brief brilliance and color and musk

you are whole
you and you alone
are more than summer laughter
and more than halcyon nights
you are more, peony, you are more.

Emily Tworek

SUMMER'S END

Solstice

crane toward the sunlight
heavy-headed peonies
look! a season's end

Boston Haskett

Second Summer Glances

apricot air casts
a temporary, white spell
between oak branches.

afternoon daydreams
laze longer than expected.
heat waves paint leaves dry.

hay fever waters
your eyes and pulses ruffle
under fingertips.

lush, goldenrod gleams
with unrestrained, baby weeds
intertwining light.

Pamela Loperena

FROM LOTUS
TO LOTUS

FALLING

Lotus

If you need love
Rest here.

In the ten thousand folds of this lotus flower
Exquisite
Fragrance will intoxicatingly
heal you.

Like the moonlight on the water
A quiet will happen here.

A tender memory
An invitation
An invisible movement
Of calm
Peace
Will bless you.

That memory in your heart
of ten thousand longings
Of sad lonely
No one is listening
Well then whisper those sorrows here.

Sublime fragrance
Of the ten thousand blossoms
Moving inward forever
Taking you in.
In this place find a home.

Fiona Pugliese

Lost Marigold

I'm looking at the marigolds
and I feel nothing

                                         – how I knew

                                                 lost
                                                 lost
                                                 lost

Macías

Maybe in a Timeline
Where Flowers are for the Living

I didn't tell you that often
but I love you,
earnestly

You used to smell of
orchids in the crsytalized rain

It's not that the scented memory
is starting to wither away,
But rather I can't remember
how to sniff a flower anymore,
without falling apart

And now I am frightened
For I could pick you
countess of red roses,
resting them on your grave

Yet they would all decay within a week,
And you are never coming back

I long to reset the clock,
To give you August sunflowers,
And see your delicate grin bloom

But that will never happen
For your garden has perished

I didn't tell you enough
but I love you,
like the dead
could have loved flowers

Maggie Kaprielian

#Atreyasverse #Autism
#Autismacceptance

Fractals rush
ideas all at once, a focus
flower spill able to choose
silence considers heart,
slip hush stream of stars
the all fight fuse
to peace hopeless
waiting for accepting touch.

Jerry Lints

The Proper Use of Honey

In younger days, my mother taught me
        about the proper use of honey.
From the time clumsy fingers
        could lift my eyes above the kitchen counter,
                I remember the line of golden jars
        (each wrapped in its own colored ribbon),
sun shining through them like stained glass.

Of the five,
        I knew four well.

Every Sunday afternoon, she called me
        to the counter, with a teaspoon
                of the green jar and lifted it to my lips.
My tongue would stick to the roof
        of my mouth until it was loosened
by the cold glass of milk she tucked into my hand.
When warm winds rolled
        through Santa Ana, kicking up dust
                and cracking my throat,
        she tipped the purple jar until gold rippled into
a hot mug of chamomile —
and after my hair transmuted
        from straight lines to unpredictable curls,
                she dipped her hand into the yellow
        and mixed it with olive oil, calming each
coil above my neck and behind my ears.
She used the blue when I was wounded,
        to seal cuts and silence scars —
the night of one Fourth of July was spent
        covering my hand,
                speckled by blisters from a sparkler,
        with honey bandages —
leaving a faint cluster I only see in certain light.

The jar wrapped in red
  evaded twenty years of questions.

On my first day of heartbreak, eyes swollen, head heavy,
  she greeted me at the counter with a rose
   she was growing outside the window,
  and twisted open the lid
through the crunching of crystals.
I watched her paint each point,
  sweetening the edges with her finger.
   "It's time that you know,"
  she said as she passed me the stem,
"the best parts of life
  are licking honey off a thorn."

Jordan Nishkian

Fine China

look inside the doorknob   tell yourself this is where love dies   that
is not the key it's stuck   you twisted it too much   you don't have
the keys to get in   there is no lock for this room   we have always
lived here   we grew this grass last summer   the lawnmower was a
gift from your mother   it is all ours   the windows the sink and the
birds   our china will never break and the cabinets will never be
empty   we will never run out of milk   the neighbors will admire
our magnolias like never before   there will be no doubts   no other
ways   you will leave me for her but when you return I will welcome
you with open doors   Daniel come Home   I will set the table for
us   don't eat just yet   there must be an attic inside me   how else
will you crawl inside this poem   the staircase will creak and I'll
know you're back.

Ayesha Bashir

28 . . .

this endless basement
in my mind
I lost myself
in the kindest lie
colors that were so fragrant
yet flowers they were not
only knotweed of my past
this fertile soil
these defiant roots
makes violent twisted pavement
tripping my solitary shadow
of a heart forever vacant
without you

Kellasandra Ferrara

WEEDS ?

Blooming

spring brings promises of rainy
days and unfurled petals,
but when a weed
overruns a garden
we don't let it ruin the
rebirth we know.
instead,
we decide what lives
and dies, what brings forth
beauty and what is
laid for ashes.
without the unchoking,
without the choice
of death and life,
our springs would be broken
and suffocated by our
own damaged hands.
instead, delicacy wins
out and paints our
world in grainy
promises
of choice over
chance and life
over loss.

Marianna Pizzini Mankle

Weeds

In early spring
before the mowing starts
the lawns are full
of dandelion gold
a sort of outlaw richness
raucous and defiant
a yellow shout
grown loud
before the work
of taming every inch
gets under way again

I must admit
I love this ragged splendor
with its stubborn grip
on survival
and its neglected virtues
that persist outside
our organized designs
humble yet
sharp toothed
deep rooted
and finally triumphant
beneath our feet

Mary McCarthy

Tiny Galaxy

Each dandelion
Lives its tiny galaxy:
Sun, then moon, then stars.

Anne E.G. Nydam

Flowers Don't Belong in Asylums

Flowers don't belong in asylums
but that didn't stop you from trying to bring them
You didn't know
they're not allowed
in case people try to eat them
You didn't know that
I didn't put myself in here to die
suicide
by flower
so the next day
you brought dandelions instead

Dandelions don't belong in asylums
you said
and neither do I

Rachel Sieff

Heliophile

In this garden,
doused in dandelion dust,
I follow the morning sun's rays.
Her ascending feelings
thaw me tender.

With two hands,
I break through soil —
shovel out dead ends and shame —
plant a seed —
waiting for sky angels to play
acoustics of rain.

Here is where I will find the remedy;
compassion stems from the deepest leaf.
When propitious vapors begin their dance,
a new blossom shall awaken slow
inside my heart space,
but uplifted as ever
for embracing self-love again —
full bloom.

Pamela Loperena

People vs. Dandelion

The council is quiet. The atmosphere is tense.
Rose says, "If you would take your seats, the trial can commence."

"Bring out the defendant. Let them speak their piece,"
Says the timid Buttercup, clearly ill-at-ease.

The council doors, they open, and I am shuffled through.
What my fate will be this day, I really wish I knew.

I am stood before the council, the beloved flowers of old.
Dahlia, Tulip, Hyacinth. Daisy, Marigold.

On each face I see disgust, just as I knew I would.
They've come this day to judge me, to decide if I am good.

"I call this trial to order," Rose says with a steel.
"Dandelion, make your case; make your last appeal.

"A flower or a weed, this is the debate.
Choose your words quite carefully, for they could seal your fate."

I clear my throat, I smooth my petals. I can hardly breathe.
If I am to live this day, I must change what they believe.

"You call me a weed, an interminable pest –
But in fact, I am a flower, and I think, one of the best."

The council starts in uproar. Tulip tries to jump the table.
But Rose holds up a steady leaf. "Continue, when you are able."

"I am strong and I am hardy. I can survive most-anything.
I stand firm in the wind when Allium is trembling.

"With my frequent flowering, I help the Pollinators.
Ha – and unlike some of you, I don't have to hide indoors.

"I thrive against the mowing, against the trials and tribulations.
I may not be the most loved – but, more than the Carnations …

"I also am quite useful — as medicine or food.
  I am highly nutritious. I can even help your mood.

"And see, I can grant wishes. Every child knows
  That my seed pods can do anything, if one only blows …"

  Impassively, Rose stands. "It is time to make our judgment."
  I watch each face intently … I wonder if I've done it.

"All in favor," Daisy asks, "of finding the defendant guilty?"
  Several leaves shoot up at once, only far too willing.

  But several leaves stay down. I turn left and right in shock.
  Tulip takes my side. Petunia. Iris. Hollyhock.

  Rose stands once more. "It seems we are divided.
  Because our votes are split, this case cannot be decided."

"We'll leave it to the Gardeners. They'll know what to do."
  Whether the Dandelion is a flower or a weed, that is up to you.

Parker Atlas Yaw

FLOWERS ILLUMINATE

Smell of Lilacs

Syringa Vulgaris Common Lilac

You keep backing up
but our faces
full of fragrance
are stuffing your mouth with green.

You want us to smell purple, delicate,
but our undulance is heavy in your lungs,
sweet turned wood turned almost sour
consuming the closed room,
masking you like a muzzle.

You step outside to breathe
and see a friend.
You step into her arms
and feel her exhale
a blue breath:

a wood plank
across a river
which you now cross.

Sierra Nelson

Weirdos

On our first date, he offers a beribboned bouquet.

Proteas.

I nuzzle their fuzzy guts.

Points for thoughtfulness, cleverness, awareness.

"I told her you're a full on weirdo so
the florist offered me the muppets."

I kiss the flower, open wide.

Dia VanGunten

Silent Watcher

I have been a silent watcher
for you will not notice me,
though I am bees within your garden
and the wind throughout your trees,
I'm the lullaby that you ignore
and so, you do not sleep,
that painful spot that you abhor,
the river that runs deep.
For every fire there's always smoke,
it's what you will not see —
the clouds and time keep rolling by,
And you belong to me.

Russelle Marcato Westbrook

Evolution

The night-blooming cereus,
Queen of the Desert, perfumes the yard,
giving her one-night-only performance.
Everyone knows this show for what it is:
an effort to employ olfactory wiles
in service of the seed, attracting
avid Sphynx moths and bats,
metallic scarabs like bouncers
in their glittering regalia.
A scent strong as a snare,
tangible as the bug-eyed peepers'
insistent shrilling in the sodden leaves.

For a week, the bud hung heavy, until
just yesterday it began to turn
up toward the light, green bodice
beginning to swell, as the double
flower prepared to meet its suitors.
Fully open now, it holds itself out
to be tasted, petals a cupped palm
nestled in a jagged ruff of lower leaves,
crowned by a yellow starburst.
As I watch, a moth's proboscis
unfurls like a fiddlehead.

Before morning, the flower will wither,
and the moon too deflate
like a day-old helium balloon.
I too play a role, as surely
smitten as the moth or beetle,
the peepers, compelled to stitch a song
out of the perfumed air.

Robbi Nester

Kin to Poison Hemlock

genus umbelliferae
hand-shaped
wanting

fists of
queen anne's
lace
fold instead
of unfold

close instead of open

grasping into fists
tight and dry
seeds hooked
with spines
the color of old lace
faded
clutching the memory
of what they were
in their verdant
prime

palm
that telltale
carmine dot
at the flower's very center
where plant gleaned
its common name
veering from latin
daucus carota
wild carrot
wild

perhaps queen anne
was wild in her
very own way

the red dot
said to be
blood
let loose
from a pinprick
when she was tatting lace

Polly Hatfield

Hawk Moth Orchid

Tonight, think of the sad, side-long embrace
of fading moonlight, a tragic arc of formless desire,
before the sun rises and the last honeyed words
of midnight viaticum dissolves on my tongue.
The sharp tenderness of old night's long sigh
leaves the drunken hawk moths dizzied from delight.
The pollen is sweeter at This hour: pollination, an
untraceable translation. All craft is in the catching
of these moments; stumbling towards daylight's
warm grasp there is nothing sweeter than a lover
laid in night gladiolus who does not know how to
name the crooks of your body but knows that they
are just the same: who knows that morning is
coming and that you will collapse into yourself
yet again and doesn't rush to devour the unnameable:
who only whispers in no language at all
the nature of love as it comes to an end.

G.E. Schwartz

Haiku

Carnation's bloom bright
providing simple beauty
in a world gone gray

Kendra Meador

Lotus From Below

lately
I've been feeling
like a lotus from below
Rising
through
the mud
Trusting
what's inside
Growing
gracefully
despite
the stuck
the sludge
the yuck
Practicing
patience
through pain
through loss
through
learning how
to love
learning how
to hold
my breath

the nudge
that if
I give
enough
if
I grow
a little
more
one day
I might
just see
the sun

Macías

BECOMING
FLOWERS

The Neglected

Alone in the serene house
books alphabetized on the shelves
the furniture all tastefully arranged
long bands of December sunlight
reach across the floor
and press against the walls

suddenly out of this quiet
a rustling movement of
vine growth
erupts upwards out of my center
twines up the back of my throat
flourishes into leaf over my tongue
and bursts forth out of my mouth

wild roots sprout from my legs
breaking through floorboards
snaking around pipes and wires
cracking the
foundation
to branch downwards into the earth

in the stunned silence
I ask, oddly *unalarmed . . . What are you?*
response: Your feral life.

Richard Shaw

Night Enchantment

Flowers in the night
turn a different color —
wet by darkness
saturated scent
reveal essence

Quicksilver morphing magic
my brain changes
my cells change.
I get bigger by
shifting into space that has no
room in the day

My skin opens
up to itself
glistens in moonlight
permeated by beauty
slowly reborn with the dew

Touching the tip of my nose
I am a saint, a fairy, a goblin, a pixie
my startled giggle
knows this is true

I in the night
turn a different color —
wet by darkness
saturated scent
essence revealed

I change with the flowers

Christina Isobel

Eventide

"You can trust people with grief,"
 she says, piecing together a bouquet
 of bee balm and blueweed.
 My fingers pick at heads of sea lavender
 I carry through tides.

Rushing sand scuffs the backs of my knees
 the way pink thrift sends fleeting scents
 of honey before swallowed by salt.

She plucks out leaves,
 brown and curling,
 tossing them into passing foam.
 Over her shoulder,

"Further."

I let my dress into the waves,
 steadying my pace, unswayed
 by the fabric's heavy ebb and flow;
 my feet trudge against grain.

Her skirt billows around her waist:
 a temporary buoyancy,
 momentary lightness.

Plumes of purple and strikes of crimson
 fall behind her. She stops
 to where our elbows graze the water
 and our toes tap sand without sinking.

She stares at the sun.
 I watch the sky burn.

My hands release, unwrap from tender stems,
 relinquishing them to the sea —

undulations meet unfurled palms.
"They'll wash back, you know."

I know.
She is more intimate with death:
tides crashing behind us,
bubbles settling on the surface,
a white-knuckled scream.

She throws her fistful overhead,
petals scattering before they hit water.

Jordan Nishkian

The Nasturtium

Last week I saw a photograph of nasturtiums.
I nostalgically thought about how in yesteryears
I planted them in my garden
to cheer me and keep me company.

But, I suppose, as things got darker
inside my house
the darkness spread to my garden
and the once robust flowers
could not survive.

Now my new life has light
and I wanted, once again,
to have nasturtiums
to smile up at me.
But it wasn't nasturtium season
so I would have to wait months
to grow them.

But I wasn't alone with my thoughts.
My dearly departed Love
is always paying attention.
Today I walked into my garden
and saw that overnight
you had somehow created
a single yellow nasturtium.
It stood tall and strong,
a tribute to your power.

I will never understand
how you do such things
from the Other Side,
but I know why you do –
it still makes you happy
to make me happy.

Vivian Imperiale

Lost and Found

Last night I missed my favorite gold chain
the one with the crab charm
we bought first time at the beach
and I took the house apart
room by room
unable to believe
it was gone

Sorting through pots and seeds
in the cellar
I found my last year's Amaryllis
there in the dark
where I'd left it cut back down
to the bulb
and forgotten

It had put up a long
pale white stem
and a huge half open
silk-red flower
disregarded
without light
without water

Resurrected from its own root
waiting for me
like a pledge
of unexpected hope

Mary McCarthy

Astraea

starry night, orchid daughter, was our first born;
a goddess in the Cupertino sun that filtered past the curtains.
Symmetry and white, unblemished petals, an apt metaphor
for relearning how to start over. I often whispered to her,
forgetting where my buds began and her father's touch ended.
I fed her with ice cubes to slow the molecules, to clarify
the liquidity of time never spent. But she only knew
what we synthesized with light reflected off our bodies
entangled like roots, off the softness of the hands you laid
on my own white petals, speckled with nothing but certainty

Elle Jay Snyder

Still a Woman

she blossomed
with no fruit to be found
beautifully barren

Jillian Calahan

Lilium

Soft and gentle.

Full of fragrant, tender beauty.

A symbol of peace.
A token of three.

Your petals part
to reveal a map to
the only place where
stigmas become soaked with nectar;

giving rise to new life.

In a chalice, brimming with
tranquility.

Courtney L. Black

A Rose, Imminent

A
No irony
All stark
And color
Rose
On a freezing day
Captured my heart
Life, rebellion
Death, imminent

ZZ Jelenic

Flower Haiku

Who has found the keys
to unlock every rose
in Bluebeard's castle?

Alexis Krasilovsky

Winter's Edge

orange-fingered flames
wrap round logs

a purple crocus
dares snow

Fay L. Loomis

Death in Hand

He tells me the bouquet is past
its prime. That may be, I say,
unbothered, I like the rot, the
tissued crepuscular phase beyond
the bloom of a brilliant evanescence,

and aren't they all brilliant? Every
tender-tongued petal, each scrolled
leaf written in the scrawl of millions
of years, the slick stems holding chin
up, even after the cut. I am rapt by the

draining color waning from peony's
febrile cheeks, the bowed head of a
tulip shattering against a tablecloth in
a pollen-peppered sigh is impressive,
if you ask me.

They are no more ashamed of dying
than a mushroom, knowing fully well
the circle never really opens to a line.
There is a twilit gasp at this hour, have
you heard it? The mouths of roses blow

velvet, unbuttoned, and I wouldn't have
them do that in the dark. I'll witness the
end, they were carved for pleasure. Oh,
he says, and takes a whiff of winsome
death in his hand.

Jessie Zechnowitz Lim

Monday, Again

And I am watering orchids,
tough beauties with few demands,
living on little more
than water, light, and air.
I carry each one to the sink
and let the water sluice through,
watching thick roots
curled down in shredded bark,
brighten to a tender green.

More rugged than their reputation,
these plants keep their own counsel,
and will bloom in their own
good time —
in colors and shapes like gifts
of an intoxicated dream
arcing into the air
like bright flags
at the gate of paradise.

Mary McCarthy

Remember

the heady scent of daphne
the kitchen door &
winter's hibernating heart
flung open to greet a new year.

deep purple clematis
small yellow narcissus
she greeted them on her knees
spring's yearly benediction.

the bounty she gathered
around her like a
young mother again
arms outstretched.

Peggy Acott

Chrysanthemum

gentle petals drop
dew onto skin, a
delicate bloom in
the eternal sun.
young and youthful,
a beauty in the short
blip of existence. the sun
strengthens, and rays grow.
petals droop then scatter –
life gone,
so short.
beauty already in the
hands of death.

Charlotte Yeung

Love, Decaying

You brought me a bouquet of chemically-preserved carnations on our first date. I kept them until they crumbled. In my journal, I sketched the stages of decay. Curling leaves, fading petals, softening stems.
Withering beauty. Beauty, withering.

The blooms came wrapped in a violet ribbon that I tied in my hair. I remember how we used to sleep draped across one another, pale and limp as wilted daisies in the summer heat. Hatless in the garden, I freckled as handsomely as your dwindling carnations, but you never noticed. My soaps and shampoo bottles sprouted like weeds in your bathroom, then vanished one by one. I began to draw you with the same attention I gave the flowers. Cold, scientific precision on the sketchbook page. The stages of our blossoming indifference.

Ella Shively

Flower Haiku

the redbud lady
under the shadow of death
blooms with a smile

Alexis Krasilovsky

After It Rains …

you plant seeds in her garden
in the backyard
beside the porch
by the rain gutter
behind the cherub statue
underneath her favorite stone
(the dark one with white specks)
and
you don't tell her.

she would get too excited

it had just rained
the air was still soft and the clouds were still tinted dark
like her white dress she stained with charcoal, building the fire inside
the soil was still damp and cold and getting stuck under your nails
she hates dirt under her nails

the rain has stopped but there are still puddles
the sun has cleared as the clouds did too
but there are still puddles of her
she calls you inside, don't get your shoes dirty
what are you doing out there anyway?

planting seeds in your garden!
but
you don't tell her that.
she'll know when it blossoms.

Samia Sayed

Snowdrops

Every year I wait to see
Snowdrops
Breaking through winter's final shell
Reaching up with threads of green
Defying cold
Defying odds
Declaring spring is possible   just when I'd begun to doubt.

Every year I wait to see
Snowdrops
Breaking through winter's final shell
Take a picture of them with my phone.

I wanted to send you the photo of
Snowdrops
Forgetting for a moment
That this year they bloom
Without you
Declaring spring is possible   just when I'd begun to doubt.

Peggy Acott

Transmogrification: A Personal Manual for Me Whose Husband is Leaving in Midlife Crisis

There is only one commandment:
You must turn into a flower.

I don't know what this means.

First the skin will
be peeled off
so my flesh
drips to the sun.
My fingernails must go
one by one.

My organs have already been treated.
but not quite.
My guts must
surely
be thronged
like the sardines
or maybe
simply rearranged.

My heart can't
be wrapped around him
any more.
My gut cannot use him
as a touchstone
anymore.
My blood cannot arise for him
any more.
Some of these things
sound good,
but I'm shaking

like the tower in the tarot.

My liver slips, spits, sputters.
There are pieces of me I
cannot name, but I
feel them move
dropping down
to rest
after their transition
as surprised
as I
by their descent.

My lungs
need to be de-glassed
from the shatter
of the heart.
Shard by shard
they need to be
surgically removed
I am told
or the splinters
can go straight to the brain.
The little cuts, spaces
are to be left
for the conversion
to chlorophyll.

And there are specific things

I must do.
Let go
Of clenching
my toes
so the flow
can gently drain
to the earth
for the formation
of roots.

The same goes
for my fists
for they must …

I must love
love more
I shout
love
in this
closing
down of love
opening open love
I must love love
only love regenerates loving
and in this loving
my fingers, my fingers will turn
to tendrils
my tongue
to pistils.

My hair
I don't know what
to do with my hair.
Shave it?
I have cut it
I look in the mirror
and I do not recognize myself.

It is beginning …
Curl it
Dye it pink.
I –

My bones?
Will they break?
Crumble?
Shatter too?
Can this process
fail
stop in media res?
Does my body
know what
to do?

And if I succeed
what will I
look like?
Will I be able
to walk?
Will I be sociable?

Will I wilt after
one day?
two?
Will this decrease
my life span?
Parts of my
brain get erased?
Studies have
shown ...
Will my friends
recognize me?
Will I be trapped
forever apart
from others?

I've been kicking
screaming
crying
shouting
fuming
foaming
falling down
beginning to love more and ...

I want to be a tuberose
a tuberose
I want to be a tuberose
I can be a —

cracking cracked apart
split splitting like a fallen
vase
I tearing rending rendering
shredding flesh falls leaving
dank smells of earth and matter
leaving
legs twisting turning turn
intertwining
tighter tighter
interweaving
tighter tight
forming stem
turning green
as life.

flower claws reach to sky
buds unfurl
scented
from the
mother mystical

flesh slips
to soft petals
touches of
pinks with
hues of blue

wet wet
all is wet
wet

Christina Isobel

Planting Daisies

If I could wrap your life in flowers,
Midnight murmurs, autumn showers,
All the strangers we've encountered,
Every minute, every hour;
Petals blue and petals green,
Every color in-between,
All the words I didn't mean,
Would you then come back to me?

If I could stop the leaves from changing,
Ban the clouds above from raining,
Shield the heart from ever breaking,
Promise you we're never aging;
Gardens fresh and gardens dead,
Thorns that grow inside our heads,
All the things we left unsaid,
Would you still be here instead?

If I could hold your hand in summer,
Skipping rocks across the river,
(Let's pretend love is for lovers,
Let's believe death only slumbers);
Roses red and roses white,
Tying the bouquet so tight,
If these flowers make things right,
Would you come to me at night?

If you can come in enter slowly,
Midnight-tulip shades of lonely
Etched upon the sheets that only
You have lain in, come and hold me.
Orchids young and orchids old,
Tell me things I do not know.
Tell me of the world below
Where people watch the flowers grow.

Nobel Chan

Rebirth

The land bears the collective traumas
     of roots wrenched up
         of stones removed

                     But every year the world moves back
                     from black and white into

bursting
Technicolor dreams
of dogwood
blossoms and pink cherry trees
lupine sun
foxgloves and columbine
     spreading through the meadow
vines climbing tendrils reaching to cover the ruins in green and soft fragrant petals
         healing over the scars, hiding the ruts in the soil, reclaiming, and
         covering the earth in blooms.

Meg Eubank

THE POETS

BLACK, COURTNEY L.

Courtney L. Black is a Cleveland-born multidisciplinary artist. Her educational background in Cultural Anthropology, Sociology, and Theater fuels her passion for connecting people from diverse backgrounds and perspectives.

As a spiritual writer, she is constantly reminded that nothing is one-dimensional. Through her multidisciplinary work, she gains a deeper understanding of self, thus a deeper understanding of others.

She is inspired by collaborative efforts that bring awareness to various social issues within the greater community. Furthermore, her artistic endeavors have strengthened her devotion to spirituality, the natural world, metaphysics, and popular culture. All of which support her through her journey of creative advocacy and BIPOC liberation.

A self-described transcendentalist, she aims not to be an artist who solely provides social commentary or observations but is proactive in using her pen and body to be an agent for true social change and community renewal.

Ms. Black's recent work includes her first self-published poetry collection titled, ANIMALIA.

Rosa p.32, Lilium p.113

BLAKELY, SARAH

Sarah Blakely (she/her) is a poet and songwriter based in California. She writes primarily about her own experiences with sexual trauma and relationships as well as struggles with mental health and healing from trauma. Her debut collection, *Volcano Girl*, as well as her second collection, *Scarlet & Shadows*, are available online through Amazon and other online booksellers. Find more of her work @sarahb.poetry on Instagram.

The Lavender Plant p.48
Previously published in her book *Volcano Girl*

BRADLEY, TYLER LENN

Tyler Lenn Bradley (she/her) is a poet, spoken word artist, and mental health advocate. Tyler strives to inspire others to thrive in the art of self-love and persevere towards their dreams with joy. Recently, Tyler's debut poetry collection *Phasing Freely*, was published by Alegria Publishing. In her book, Tyler explores her personal mental health journey through the many phases of the moon, inviting readers to excavate and examine the craters of their own. Tyler's poetry has a global footprint, having traveled and performed throughout the United States, Italy, France, England, Ireland, Spain, and Australia. Her work transcends borders, touching hearts and inspiring minds wherever she goes. Tyler's poetry graces the pages of various national and international anthologies, and she is host of the Los Angeles Poet Society's "Voices of Color" Instagram Live which serves to amplify the voices and stories of BIPOC poets. When not immersed in the world of poetry, Tyler is a live entertainment Creative Producer for the world's most beloved theme parks. You can contact or follow Tyler's poetry journey through her Instagram @TylerLennBradley and website TylerLennBradley.com.

Ant Advice p.62

CALAHAN, JILLIAN
Jillian Calahan is a poet and short story writer from the Pacific Northwest. When she's not writing she can be found lost in a bookstore, hanging out with her four cats and two dogs, doing crafts, or taking too many pictures of pretty sunsets. You can find her on Instagram @novamarie_poetry

Still A Woman p.112

CERNY, JANA
As a native Californian, witnessing nature has been my spiritual life force since day one. I am a mother, dancer, teacher, natural perfumer and sporadic poet. Having recently relocated to Oregon I am falling in love with all the new flora and fauna.

Peony Attempts p.58

CHAN, NOBEL
Nobel Chan is a junior at Boston University studying English and Deaf Studies. Hailing from Hong Kong, she loves to read, write, and sing. Her work has been published in anthologies such as *Fool's Honor* and *Aphotic Love*. She hopes to continue writing more fiction and poetry in the future.

Planting Daisies p.128

COWGILL, COURTNEY LOWERY

Courtney Lowery Cowgill writes from a small farm on the central Montana plains in the shadow of the Rocky Mountain Front. She also teaches writing and journalism at the University of Montana School of Journalism and is pursuing her master's degree in nonfiction at Johns Hopkins University. She is currently working on a collection about loss, land and finding home, or not.

Parts of Us p.54

DREISTADT, NIKI

Niki Dreistadt has had a hilarious and truly unique career as stagehand, storyteller and farmer. You can find her published work in *Thumbnail Magazine:6* (Prosopon) and in an upcoming sci-fi podcast mini series produced by Ngano Press (*Unlivable Worlds*). She has performed with The Chicago Neofuturists, Chicago Dramatists, Salonathon, Toronto Sketch Festival and Chicago Sketch Festival. Niki Dreistadt currently works as an urban farmer and volunteer coordinator for Chicago Patchwork Farms and is a freelancer based in Chicago, Illinois.

Gathered~Wilted p.21

ENGEL, BOB

Bob Engel is a psychotherapist and former actor, chef, mushroom grower gardening in Sonoma County.

Late Summer p.56

EUBANK, MEG

Meg Eubank is a poet, teacher, photographer, and artist from Bucks County, Pennsylvania and grew up in a town aptly named Gardenville. She has been published in a number of literary magazines and other publications and has performed at countless open mic nights. She has had work in *Modern Romantic Magazine, Quail Bell Magazine, The Allegheny Review, The Original Magazine, Marathon Literary Review*, and was featured in an interview about teaching poetry on the NCTE (National Council for Teachers of English) blog. Meg has been the editor of several zines and art magazines, including *Gargoyle Art and Literary Magazine, Mosaic Art and Lit Zine, Glenside Artists and Writers*, and *The Fridge Door*.

Rebirth p.129

FENALD, ANASTASIA HELENA

Anastasia Helena Fenald is a second-generation Ukrainian-Latinx-American poet from Los Angeles and the Mojave Desert. She has a B.A. in Global Studies from the University of Riverside, California (2014) and an M.A. in Globalization and Development from the University of Sheffield, United Kingdom (2015). She spends most of her free time attending poetry workshops, performing at local open mics, and exploring Southern California. Her first poetry collection *Help Me, I'm Here: Poems to Myself*, was published by the World Stage Press in July 2022. She has also been published in *Sheila-Na-Gig Online Journal, Acid Verse Literary Journal, The Sims Library of Poetry's Anthology Poems in Praise of Libraries*, and *innate*DIVINTY books' anthology *A Case for the Personhood of Trees* and more.

Of Hummingbirds and Fairy Trees p.24

FERRARA, KELLASANDRA

Kellasandra Ferrara is a former restauranteur and baker who has been jotting down recipes, lyrics and musings forever but finally decided to subject herself onto an unwilling audience.

The current offerings of Poetry are mostly Heartbreak and Lost Love and the Novel and Short Stories are Psychological Crime Thrillers. The Cookbook is still on a perpetual shelf but she is happy to help with any cooking fiasco.

She actually cracks herself up though, she's a pretty happy person.

28 ... p.81

FRANCO, DAISY

Daisy Franco was born and raised in Chicago, Illinois. She enjoys writing poetry, fiction, and nonfiction. Her work has been published in *Chicken Soup for the Soul: Dreams and Premonitions, Chicken Soup for the Soul: Inspiration for Teachers, Mural Magazine, Puro Chicanx Writers of the 21st Century*, and the online anthology *Love You Madly*. She received her undergraduate degree from the University of Illinois at Chicago and holds a graduate degree from DePaul University.

Listening to Roses p.41

FU, JEANELLE

Jeanelle Fu is a Taiwanese-American creative writer who resides in Los Angeles. She graduated with a bachelor in English Literature from UCLA. Her debut poetry collection *Blueprints* has been featured by Taiwanese-American.org, Yu & Me books, and Pon Ding bookstore in Taipei. She also does custom poetry & watercolor prints at local pop ups.

Scent of a Memory p.51

GREENE, TOVA

Tova Greene (they/them) is a non-binary, queer, Jewish poet who recently graduated with a bachelor in liberal arts from Sarah Lawrence college in Yonkers, New York. they were one of seven members of the class of 2022 to submit a senior thesis; at a whopping 375 pages, "the poetic is political" specialized in the inter-section between twentieth century American poetry & feminist theory. as a part of this year-long endeavor, they created a chronological anthology of the American feminist poetry movement from 1963-1989 entitled who can tolerate the power of a woman (after "propaganda poem: maybe for some young mamas" by Alicia Ostriker). they are currently producing the New York city poetry festival. their work has been featured in *eunoia review, midway journal, love & squalor, clickbait, soul talk magazine, & primaverazine*. they currently live in Manhattan with their partner & cat. for inquiries, please reach out to tova@poetrysocietyny.org.

Lavender on My Forehead on Ash Wednesday p.23

HATFIELD, POLLY

Polly Hatfield calls Portland, Oregon home. Her back fence borders an old pioneer cemetery and she remains grateful for the quiet. Her words have been published in *Fire and Rain: Ecopoetry of California*. She shares a bountiful parcel of land with her partner and one beloved striped cat.

Peony Revelry p.60, Kin to Poison Hemlock p.96

HASKETT, BOSTON

Boston Haskett obtained an MFA in creative writing from the University of Washington in 2020. Boston currently lives in the Pacific Northwest and enjoys spending time with family, learning about farming flowers, and of course writing.

Transmutation p.27, Solstice p.68

HILL, RACHEL

Rachel Hill lives in Seattle, Washington. She earned her MFA from the University of Washington and has served as an editor for *Poetry Northwest Editions* & the *Seattle Review*.

From the Shakespeare Garden p.53

IMPERIALE, VIVIAN

Vivian Imperiale has been looking at the world with a poet's eye since she was six. She lives in San Francisco surrounded by flower gardens.

The Nasturtium p.109

JELENIC, ZZ

ZZ Jelenic is a Ukrainian-born poet raised in New York City and New Jersey. She lives in New Jersey with her husband and their two daughters.

Odessa Flowers p.11, *A Rose, Imminent* p.114, *Joy Flower* p.155

JOHNS, DEIRDRE GARR

Deirdre Garr Johns resides in South Carolina with her family. Nature is an inspiration, and poetry is a first love. Much of her work is inspired by memories of people and places. Her poetry has appeared in *Sylvia* magazine, *South Carolina Bards Poetry Anthology*, and *Eunoia Magazine*. Her nonfiction work has been published by the Surfside Chapter of the South Carolina Writers Association and *Sasee Magazine*. Her website is amuseofonesown.com.

Our Losses Are Softened p.37

JOHNSON, KIKI

Kiki Johnson is a native New Yorker exiled to Florida. She has an MFA in Creative Writing from the New School, which infuses her work as a freelance copy editor and writing coach. Her work is published in *thread litmag, BarBar, New Note Poetry Magazine, The Winged Moon Magazine, The Autores Weekly, Mars Hill Review*, and *Image Journal*. Poems based on her trauma recovery journey are featured in *Phoenixes: an anthology written by survivors*.
@kiki poetry

While Listening to Love Supreme p.13, *The Power of Roses* p.42

JUREK, ADRIANNA

Adrianna is a transplant New Yorker, writer, and visual artist. She lives her life like a cat with nine lives, and she is sometimes lonely in a room full of people.

A Brief Romantic Daydream p.38

KAPRIELIAN, MAGGIE

Maggie Kaprielian is an 18-year-old poet from Maryland. She's a freshman at Emerson College studying writing, literature and publishing. When not studying or working for her school's publications, she can be found wandering Boston with friends.

Maybe in a Timeline Where Flowers Are for the Living p.76

KOLBER, SAMANTHA

Samantha Kolber is an award-winning poet published in *Rattle, Mom Egg Review, Hunger Mountain, The Meadow,* and other journals and anthologies. Her chapbook *Birth of a Daughter* (Kelsay Books, 2020) won the 2021 Human Relations Indie Book Award in Realistic Poetry. She received an MFA from Goddard College and completed post-grad studies in poetry at Pine Manor College's Solstice MFA Program. Originally from New Jersey, she lives in Montpelier, Vermont, near a peony farm.

Peony Double Etheree p.59

KRASILOVSKY, ALEXIS

Alexis makes poetry films. Her most recent film, *The Parking Lot of Dreams,* is a hybrid of poetry and photocollages, some of which also appear in her new book, *Watermelon Linguistics: New and Selected Poems* (Cyberwit: India, 2022). She is also the author of the book *Great Adaptations: Screenwriting and Global Storytelling* (Routledge: 2nd place winner of .the 2019 International Writers' Awards), and co-author of *Shooting Women: Behind the Camera, Around the World* (Intellect Books/U Chicago Press, 2015). She studied at Yale and CalArts, and lives in Los Angeles.

For more information, see https://alexiskrasilovsky.com.

Flower Haiku p.115, Flower Haiku p.122

LANZONE, GLORIA S.

Gloria S. Lanzone is a writer whose poems and short stories have been published in the Bronx Memoir Project, Volumes III, IV, V and VI, VII and NYT Metropolitan Diary. Her focus is on the inspirational, nonfiction, & memoir marketplace. She is currently working on her memoir.

Pink Carnations p.49

LIM, JESSIE ZECHNOWITZ

Jessie Zechnowitz Lim is a florist by day and poet by night living in the San Francisco Bay Area (on unceded Lisjan Ohlone land). She holds an MA and BA in Art History with an AA in English from San Francisco State University, UC Berkeley, and San Diego City College respectively. Her work has been published or is forthcoming in *Litbreak Magazine, The Bold Italic*, and *Mother Mag*.

Me-Nots p.12, Wisteria p.46, Death in Hand p.117

LINTS, JERRY

I'm 65, and have lived 40 years in San Francisco, CA. I have one daughter. First published in a *World of Poetry* anthology 1979 Sacramento, CA.

#Atreyasverse #Autism #Autismacceptance p.77

LOMBRÉ, SUNSHINE

Southside Chicago native Sunshine Lombré is a dancer & poet who specializes in expressing sensuality & emotional authenticity through her words & movements. Sunshine performs poetry and choreography throughout the Midwest Area while also curating seasonal artist showcases based around Black heritage. Sunshine strives to share her passion for Spoken Word and choreography while uplifting Black communities worldwide through teaching creative writing classes through "Poetry for Personal Power," the Chicago Public Library system and other arts organizations. She's been an opening act for Twista and has recently released her debut poetry album called *Fading Away*.

Mademoiselle Neon Noir p.47

LOOMIS, FAY L.

Fay L. Loomis lives a particularly quiet life in the woods in upstate Kerhonkson, New York. A member of the Stone Ridge Library Writers and Rat's Ass Review Workshop, her poetry and prose appear in numerous publications, including most recently in *Rat's Ass Review, Amethyst Review, Mad Swirl, Stick Figure Poetry, Breath and Shadow* and *Hindsight*.

Winter's Edge p.116

LOPERENA, PAMELA

Pamela Loperena is a 23-year-old writer from New York. She is a graduate of SUNY New Paltz with a major in Psychology and minors in Creative Writing and Deaf Studies. Her pieces have appeared in *The Teller Magazine* and *Inkling* as well as other publications. When she isn't penning poetic works, she's drowning in fictitious novel pages or listening to the latest indie tunes.

Lovestruck p.35, Second Summer Glances p.69, Heliophile p.88

MACÍAS

A classically trained vocalist, poet, and international teaching artist. Founder of @OneSoundEarth, she has dedicated her life to exploring the interdependence of the human voice, identity, epigenetics, and the environment. She teaches the importance of and means for using the voice as a way of healing one's relationship to Self, the collective, and the environment. Singing is her first form of loving self-expression. Poetry is a close second.

Lost Marigold p.75, Lotus From Below p.100

MANKLE, MARIANNA PIZZINI

Marianna Pizzini Mankle is a Montana native who now calls Nebraska home. She loves to read, write, and serve at church. She is studying for an MA in Communication at Arizona State University. Her writing can be found in *Kiosk, Calla Press,* and *Writeresque Literary Magazine*. When she isn't writing, she can be found watching reality TV with her husband.

Blooming p.84

MEADOR, KENDRA

Kendra Meador lives and works in Idaho as an artist and writer. Her preferred art mediums are acrylics, colored pencils, pastels, and photography.

Poetry and essays are her primary forms of literary art. Creating art is her way of honoring our human experience and revealing our connection with nature. Kendra also enjoys baking, gardening, and spending time with her husband and two teenage boys.

Haiku p.99

MCCARTHY, MARY
Mary McCarthy is a retired Registered Nurse who has always been a writer. Her work has appeared in many journals and anthologies, including *The Ekphrastic World,* edited by Lorette Luzajic, *The Plague Papers.* Edited by Robbi Nester, and recent issues of *Earth's Daughters* and *Third Wednesday.* She has been a Pushcart and Best of the Net nominee.

Weeds p.85, Monday, Again p.118, Lost and Found p.110
Weeds previously published in *Third Wednesday. Lost and Found* previously published in *Verse Virtual*

MOORE, DANIEL ABDAL-HAYY
Born in 1940 in Oakland, California, Daniel Abdal-Hayy Moore had his first book of poems, *Dawn Visions,* published by Lawrence Ferlinghetti of City Lights Books, San Francisco, in 1964, and the second in 1972, *Burnt Heart/Ode to the War Dead.* In 2011, 2012 and 2014 he was a winner of the Nazim Hikmet Prize for Poetry. In 2013 he won an American Book Award, and in 2013 and 2014 was listed among The 500 Most Influential Muslims for his poetry.

If All the Wood in the World p.39
From *In the Realm of Neither* published by Ecstatic Exchange 2008

NELSON, SIERRA
Sierra Nelson's books include *The Lachrymose Report* (Poetry NW Editions) and *I Take Back the Sponge Cake* (Rose Metal Press) collaborating with visual artist Loren Erdrich. Her poems have been published in journals such as *Pleiades, Gulf Coast, Crazyhorse,* and *Poetry Northwest.* She lives in Seattle. For more information: songsforsquid.tumblr.com

After Rilke's Roses p.14, Smell of Lilacs p.92
After Rilke's Roses was first printed in *The Lachrymose Report* (Poetry NW Editions, 2018)

NESTER, ROBBI

Robbi Nester lives and writes in Southern California. She is the author of four books of poetry and editor of three anthologies. Her poetry and reviews are widely published. Learn more at her website: robbinester.net.

Evolution p.95
Evolution first appeared in her book, *Other-Wise* (Kelsey, 2017)

NISHKIAN, JORDAN

Jordan Nishkian is an Armenian-Portuguese writer based in California. Her prose and poetry explore themes of duality and have been featured in national and international publications. She has been awarded the Rollick Magazine Fiction Prize and has been nominated for the Pushcart Prize and Best American Short Stories. Jordan is the Editor-in-Chief of *Mythos* literary magazine and author of *Kindred*, a novella.

The Proper Use of Honey p.78, Eventide p.107

NYDAM, ANNE E.G.

Anne E.G. Nydam has been writing poems and creating imaginary worlds since she could hold a crayon, bringing pictures to life in both art and writing. A former middle school art teacher with an undergraduate degree in linguistics, she makes relief block prints celebrating the wonders of worlds both real and imaginary, and writes books about adventure, creativity, and looking for the best in others. More at: nydamprints.com Instagram: @nydamprints

Bee and Rose p.44, Tiny Galaxy p.86

OBREGON, TARA

Tara Obregon is an artist, composer and writer that resides in Monterey, CA. Since a young age, she has written short stories, poetry and composed music. She recently released an instrumental album about Big Sur (*Through Beauty and Terror*) which is the place that gave her the hope and purpose to pursue writing her stories, in both poetry and music.

The Lover's Melody p.36

ORPI, IRIS

(she/her) A Filpina writer currently living in Chicago. She is the author of the illustrated novel *The Espresso Effect*, four poetry collections, and five films, including the award-winning *Sons and Brothers*. She was nominated for the Pushcart Prize for Poetry in 2018.

Mizuage p.18

PANKIW, KRISTYN LEE

Kristyn Lee Pankiw holds a bachelor of arts degree in English from Flagler College. She is the author of two poetry collections, *Sunlight Through the Cracks* (April 2020), and *Teeth Kiss* (June 2020) and her writing has been published in *Comestible Journal, Good News Paper*, and *Plants are Magic Magazine*. Two of her poems, *Watermelon* and *Orange*, received the Shepherdstown Poem of the Month award, and she has been a featured poet at a few live events including Left of the Bank: A Magical Evening of Music and Poetry. She lives in Los Angeles and currently writes a digital newsletter called *Dollhouse Musings*.

The Flower Shop p.3, An Offering p.25, Happy Again p.52

PUGLIESE, FIONA

Poetic Musè Grateful spirit in a material world. Alive and well on the island of Kaua'i. Inspired by bird songs my devotion is the liquid aquamarine sea I thrive in daily. My urge is to offer direct contact with the natural world through my prose.

Lotus p.74

REDDIN, GARY

Gary Reddin grew up in Southwest Oklahoma among the cicada songs and tornado sirens. His writing was born in this dissonance. He holds an MFA from Lindenwood University. His work has most recently appeared in *Cathexis Northwest Press, The Dillydoun Review*, and *Bright Flash Literary Magazine*. His chapbook *An Abridged History of American Violence* was published in 2019 through Rose Rock Press.

Pink Camelias p.20

SAYED, SAMIA

I am Samia Sayed, a 17-year-old student from Southern California. I am a junior in high school, and with the stress of this tough academic year, writing poetry has been an incredibly important outlet for me, especially coming back from lockdown and Covid-19. As a kid, I always enjoyed creative writing as a way to express myself, and my perception of the world around me.

In my time away from writing, I find a sense of community in choral singing and NJROTC. I also enjoy spending time in nature, watching the birds, caring for my succulents, and listening to all kinds of music, including Taylor Swift and Ben Platt. Being a young South Asian woman, I have always been passionate about inclusion, diversity, and representation of writing that communicates the unique experiences of people from all different backgrounds.

After it Rains ... p.123

SCHWARTZ, G.E.

G. E. Schwartz is the author of *Only Others Are* (Legible Press), *Murmurations* (Foothills Press), *The Very Light We Reach For* (Legible Press), and lives in upstate New York.

Jasmine p.50, Hawk Moth Orchid p.98

SHARMA, DIVYANKA

Divyanka loves to use the magic of words to represent the world around her, ranging from her native country of India to her adopted home in the United States. Her poetry, fiction, and thought pieces have appeared in print and online magazines like *the other side of hope, Empyrean, Muse India, Wire.in*, among others. She hopes her writing can transport readers to feelings and places they long for. She lives in San Francisco.

Flowers in Bloom p.7

SHAW, RICHARD

Richard Shaw lives in the Connecticut River Valley of Massachusetts where he resides in a pear orchard on Horse Mountain, above Haydenville.

A former dancer and choreographer, he maintains a private practice as a Rolfer®. His poems have appeared in journals both in the United States and abroad, including *Blue Lyra*, *The Galway Review* and *Hummingbird*. He is the author of *The Orchard House* (Antrim House Books, 2019).

Residence in the Rain p.22, Rose p.33, The Neglected p.105
These three poems were originally published in *The Orchard House* (Antrim House Books, 2019)

SHIVELY, ELLA
Ella Shively is a writer and wildlife technician from La Crosse, Wisconsin. Her work has been published in *Runestone, Prometheus Dreaming, Bracken*, and elsewhere. You can find her on Instagram @shivelywrites.

Love, Decaying p.121

SIEFF, RACHEL
Rachel Sieff is a neurodivergent storyteller based in New York City. Over time, what started out as a byproduct of being born with a sleeping disorder cultivated the unique creative perspective from which she now draws inspiration — her dreams. Due to also being ADD, and the hyperfixations that come with it, her approach to storytelling is not defined by genre, style or medium. She utilizes various forms of art, music and language to share the vivid dreams and hallucinations that plague her consciousness, and highlight her experiences as a neurodivergent woman.

Flowers Don't Belong in Asylums p.87

SLOAN, ANGELA
Angela Sloan received her MA in English and Creative Writing from Longwood University; she now lives and writes in New York City. Her previous works have been published by Three Rooms Press, Genre: Urban Arts, and A Gathering of the Tribes; her chapbook, *Stories About Love* was published in 2021.

Pink Peony p.61
Previously published in the summer 2022 issue of *Mandarin Magazine* based in Chico, CA.

SNYDER, ELLE JAY

Elle Jay Snyder (they/them) is a queer performance artist and Pushcart — nominated poet from Staten Island. They have helped facilitate a poetry workshop for youth as a volunteer at the Staten Island LGBQ Center. They were a member of the 2018 Advanced Slam Team that competed in NPS. They are the author of the chapbook *Where the Knife Landed* from NYSAI Press. They have also been buried alive for the Queer Van Kult: Revelation exhibit in the name of queer art. Their words can be found most recently in *Veneralia*, an anthology from Lupercalia Press and are forthcoming in an anthology from great weather for MEDIA.

Astrea p.111

TWOREK, EMILY

Emily Tworek (she/her) is a writer living in New York City. At her day job, she works in nonprofits. In her creative work, she writes fiction, poetry, and is a co-founder of Twice Rolled Tales, a TTRPG studio focused on telling character-driven, unexpected stories. She also loves to cook, care for her houseplants, and explore nature in New York and beyond. Emily's fiction and writing for stage have received numerous awards, and can be read on her website, emilytworek.com.

Peony p.64

VAN GUNTEN, DIA

Dia VanGunten hopes to blur the boundary between poetry/prose, between real living flowers/cultural representations of flowers.

Floral Energy p.17, Weirdos p.93

VAN GUNTEN, ZOE

Zoe VanGunten reads and writes in Toledo, El Rito, Tierra Amarilla, Austin, Sevilla, Pamplona, Santa Fe — always on the bus at the last minute and always happiest at a window. Zoe's poems are short and musical, often intended to fit into song and almost always bilingual. One such "song" was shortlisted for the Montreal International Poetry Prize and appeared in print in its English form. Zoe's biggest dream is to publish her works as they were intended — as bilingual English/Spanish poems.

March Fourteenth p.26

WESTBROOK, RUSSELLE MARCATO

I am a visual artist but my writing has never been published. I am fascinated by light versus dark, life versus death and purity vs. depravity as there is never one without the other. I have a website: russellebluerose.com

Silent Watcher p.94

WONG, VALERIE

Valerie Wong (Instagram: @theglutenfreepoet) was born in Toronto, raised in Hong Kong and lives in New York. As a Third Culture Kid, she is a local and a foreigner wherever she goes. Her poetry has been published by journals and anthologies around the world, including Stanford University's *Mantis*, the League of Canadian Poets and New Zealand's Blackmail Press. She is currently seeking representation for her debut romance novel, *The Sweetest Deal.*

Roses p.34

YAW, PARKER ATLAS

Parker Atlas Yaw is a junior at SUNY Potsdam, and they are majoring in English, Education, and Anthropology. They have been writing creatively since they were in sixth grade, and they are more comfortable with cats than with people. They are incredibly socially awkward and would very much like to change the subject.

People vs. Dandelion p.89

YEUNG, CHARLOTTE

Charlotte Yeung is the 2022 Youth Poet Laureate, an Amazon Best-selling Author, an illustrator, and a foodie. She wrote and illustrated *Isabelle and the Magic Bird* and *Coloring Climate Justice.* She is a junior at Purdue University.

Chrysanthemum p.120

THE BOOK MAKERS

ISOBEL, CHRISTINA: *publisher, editor, curator, poet*
Poet. Performer. Bookmaker. Lyric playwright. Mother. Grammy. Author of the play *Skeleton Woman* and poetry/art book *Everyday Mermaid* with art by Deidre Scherer. Created and produced multi-media poetry and Indian dance concerts for Robert Bly. Poetry featured in *Pivot & Pause: An Anthology* by Azure Antoinette and Elizabeth Gilbert.

CEO of *a thousand flowers books*. Served on the board of O'Reilly Media and was influential in shaping its foundational and cultural values.

To The Flower Garden p 28, Night Enchantment p.106,
Transmogrification p.125

BLYTH, TRINITY: *assistant editor, curator, submission compilation*
Currently creative director at *a thousand flowers books*. Started her career as a producer at CNN. Worked in San Francisco for many years advising start-up technology companies on media strategy and storytelling. Documentary film producer. Studied journalism at the University of Montana and New York University.

ACKNOWLEDGEMENTS

CHRISTINA ISOBEL

First and foremost my daughters *Meara O'Reilly* and *Arwen O'Reilly Griffith* who believe in my work and tell me their truths. And *Arwen* for the final proofing of the book.

Gina Blaber, dear friend who reads everything no matter how busy she is and gives me honest feedback.

Jana Cerny who listens to my nervousness and trusts my creativity.

Deidre Scherer always after having created *Everyday Mermaid* together.

Collaborators *Trinity Blyth* and *Monique Comacchio* for the long hours and dedication to beauty/detail and laughter.

Trinity our date keeper.

Lori Bloustein life coach/therapist for her constant practical support in design elements and launching this book into the world.

Vera Kober for letting us use her beautiful artwork and her lovely comments about the cover.

All the poets for their submissions.

Flowers which always bring me happiness.

And to this project. It brings me great joy.

TRINITY BLYTH

To my son, *Ian Caldwell* for being such a wonderful human being and inspiring me to work on projects that matter.

Courtney Lowery Cowgill for copy editing this book. And for being my collaborator since college and always believing in me.

Christina Isobel and *Monique Comacchio* for teaching me so much about poetry and book design.

Lila Martin DeBenedetti for your editorial consulting. Your work on this book made it so much better.

a thousand flowers

Rooted in the natural world, we are a women-led independent publishing company. Our poetry books offer immersive, embodied experiences for a more direct connection to ourselves, others, and the earth.

We wish to expand the diversity and reach of our books to weave connections between people, create more opportunities for our poets, and expand the range and number of poetry readers around the world.

Poetry nourishes the soul, heart, and mind. For us the underbelly of much poetry is ecstatic, mystic – celebrating beauty and love, while acknowledging life's hard truths. Our wish is for more people to experience this gift – particularly in these troubled times.

WHEN FLOWERS SING was designed by Monique Comacchio of Studio Ephemera for *a thousand flowers books*. The cover artwork was painted by Vera Kober and photographed by Bill Morrison. The book was set in Spectrum, a typface designed by Jan van Krimpen in 1943, then later published by Monotype. The typeface was designed to be used in a Bible of the Spectrum publishing house in Utrecht. The project was cancelled, but the typeface was completed by Monotype in London.

Joy Flower

Joy!

Joy!   Joy!
Joy!   Joy!
Joy!   Joy!
Joy!   Joy!
Joy! Joy! Joy! Joy! Joy! Joy!
Joy! Joy! Joy! Joy! Joy! Joy! Joy!
Joy! Joy! Joy! Joy! Joy!
Joy! Joy! Joy! Joy!
Joy! Joy! Joy! Joy!
Joy! Joy! Joy!
Joy!
Joy!
Joy!
Joy!
Joy!
Joy!
Joy!
Joy!
Joy!
Joy!
Joy!
Joy!

ZZ Jelenic

Printed in the USA
CPSIA information can be obtained
at www.ICGtesting.com
LVHW020027290824
789291LV00001B/1